TIME TO DIVIDE AMERICA

by *Carl Fest*

Dorrance Publishing Co
585 Alpha Drive
Suite 103
Pittsburgh, PA 15238
Visit our website at *www.dorrancebookstore.com*

ISBN: 979-8-88729-024-9
EISBN: 979-8-88729-524-4

TIME TO
DIVIDE AMERICA

CHAPTER 1
The Challenge That Faces Us

Well before the 2020 election, the friction between Blues and Reds was evident. And the current divisions, while perhaps heightened by the actions of individuals, were symptomatic of basic differences.

These differences between the two communities, Blue and Red (particularly on the fringes), are now so fundamentally opposite on so many key issues—race, law enforcement, immigration, healthcare, taxation, family and reproduction, sexual identity, gun control, and the economy to name a few—that compromise may be unachievable. As one side progresses on their agenda, the other side perceives nothing but loss.

As an example, around the time of the 2022 primaries, MSNBC reported that a Colorado Republican candidate for governor sought to have the state do away with the popular vote in which all votes are equal and replace it with an electoral college that would give more voting power to rural counties where Republicans perform better.[1]

Debates about removing the senate filibuster rule as well as fights over redistricting and voting practices are merely examples of wasted energy spent in seeking ways to confound the opposition and unilat-

---

[1] Kyle Clark, "GOP candidate for Colorado governor says eliminate one-person, one-vote system," https://www.9news.com, May 18,2022, https://www.9news.com/article/news/local/next/lopez-gop-candidate-colorado-governor-eliminate-one-person-vote-electoral-college/73-2caf357d-aa42-4cef-abae-ac5795bb46c6

erally impose decisions on others. These efforts result in distractions from dealing with serious problems that face us.

And the costs to taxpayers can be substantial. Pennsylvania, my own state, reported a significant amount of money was spent in legal fees related to challenges to the 2020 election.[2] This is money that could have been better spent addressing critical issues.

One study indicated that 40% of all Americans feel the country is going in the wrong direction. I suggest that regardless of the outcome of recent or future elections, that percentage will not change.

Shortly after his re-election in 2020, Kentucky senator, Mitch McConnell, remarked that "our fellow citizens are not our enemies."[3] But in fact, for many on both sides of the divide, the opposition is seen as a threat and a roadblock to their vision of what they want America to be and become. And those elected to offices, especially legislative and executive offices, are perceived to represent only the interests of those constituents who voted for them.

Legislation in many states imposing voting restrictions is explained by legislatures as acts to ensure voting integrity even if no need for such legislation has been proven. It is clear that we are no longer in an era where political parties seek to persuade voters of the rightness of their views. Instead, we have moved to an age when each party will do almost anything it can to retain power.

From the protests and demonstrations, it has become very clear that there are two primary visions of what America should be. I believe it is equally clear that Blues and Reds do not wish to live in the America the other seeks to foster. And in many cases, there are those who do not wish to share their America with those of the other group.

One can even find cases of divisions in individual households. And

---

2 Julia Agos, "Taxpayers footed Pa.'s bill for election lawsuits. Costs went into the millions," https://www.pennlive.com, Apr. 14, 2021, https://www.pennlive.com/news/2021/04/taxpayers-footed-pas-bill-for-election-lawsuits-costs-went-into-the-millions.html

3 Josh James, "McConnell After Election Win: 'Our Fellow Citizens Are Not Our Enemies,'" https://www.wuky.org, November 3, 2020, https://www.wuky.org/post/mcconnell-after-election-win-our-fellow-citizens-are-not-our-enemies#stream/0

in some cases, these divisions have even led to bitter disputes and rejection of family members and once-close friends. Some have even speculated that the division could break democracy or even lead to real civil disorder and large-scale violence.

The political result, both at the state and federal levels, is often gridlock or even policy reversals based on who wins elections. Going forward, gridlock or worse, social unrest and violence, are not viable options if we wish to continue as a prosperous and secure society.

In his 1996 Book, *The Tenth Insight*, James Redfield wrote about what he believed would come to pass in American society, "great numbers of people seemed to be gravitating to one perspective or the other (what I am referring to here as blue and red), with both sides raising the stakes to that of war, of good vs. evil, and both visualizing the other as the perpetrators of a grand conspiracy."[4]

In April of 2022, the reporter, Julia Davis reported American intelligence officials had determined, that Russia's efforts to interfere in the country's election processes, was never limited to boosting any particular candidates, but rather aimed to harm America as a whole." She quoted Dmitry Drobnitsky, a Russian political scientist specializing in US affairs, as saying, "With Europe, economic wars should take priority. With America, we should be working to amplify the divisions and—in light of our limited abilities—to deepen the polarization of American society."[5] If this is true, this is one more reason to determine a way through the impasse.

I believe the nation can be seen as consisting of three types of communities—urban areas, suburbs, and rural areas/small towns. Each has its own culture, own challenges, and own problems. For the most part, the urban areas and coastal areas voted overwhelming blue in the 2020 election, while most rural areas and small towns as well as most Heart-

---

[4] James Redfield, The Tenth Insight, 1998, Warner Books, page 131

[5] Julia Davis, "Russia Airs its Ultimate 'Revenge Plan' for America, The Daily Beast, April 11, 2022, https://www.thedailybeast.com/russian-state-media-airs-its-ultimate-revenge-plan-for-2024-us-presidential-elections

land and Southern states voted overwhelmingly red. Suburbs appear to be mixed, based on location and demographics.

If we examine a map of that election, it can be noted that even in states that voted for one presidential or congressional candidate or the other, there were pockets of blue in states that voted red and pockets of red within states that voted blue.

For generations, school children have learned that representatives of the original colonies held the first Continental Congress in 1774 in opposition to British policies.[6] This was the first time that the colonies had united around a common cause.

The grand experiment that followed resulted in the Articles of Confederation. Although self-governing models were already in existence in Switzerland and Iceland for example, nothing of this scale had been tried before this experiment in democratic government.

However, shortly after the Revolutionary War, the limitations of the model led the new states to explore an alternative for governing the new nation. Despite the fact that it was clear to many that a more federal approach was needed, opposition to the new constitution was fierce.

The Anti-federalists feared that the new national government would be too powerful and would threaten individual liberties. Nevertheless, the Federalists won out and the Constitution as we know it was ratified in 1788. We have lived under this experiment ever since with periodic amendments that continued to modify and evolve it. But perhaps the current conflicts and acrimony warrant a look at a different approach.

It is worth noting that during the Constitutional Convention, Thomas Jefferson had gone on record, much to the distress of the other delegates, saying that a new constitutional convention might be necessary every twenty years or so.[7]

The American Revolution has often been termed an evolution rather than a revolution. It did not upend everything that was in place,

[6] Paul Johnson, <u>A History of the American People</u>, 1998, Harper Perennial, page 147

[7] Seymour Morris Jr, <u>American History Revised</u>, 2010, Broadway Books, page 273

such as occurred in the French and Russian Revolutions, but built on it. The following proposal would do the same.

What if both Reds and Blues could have their America within one country without talk of secession or violent conflict? I suggest that the time has come to examine at least one alternative for the nation. In the following chapters, I am presenting that alternative and its possible ramifications. This alternative focuses on how we could have two separate entities within one united nation. These entities would focus on internal (i.e., domestic) political, social, and economic concerns while continuing to address truly national concerns collectively and providing a united front for international challenges and priorities.

CHAPTER 2
A Possible Model

As stated in the Tenth Amendment to the Constitution, "all powers not delegated to the United States by the Constitution, nor prohibited by it to the States, are reserved to the States respectively, or to the people."[8] In effect, this divides the governing of the nation between the federal government and the states. But what if there were a third element that could claim some of the powers of the federal government and some of the powers held by the states?

Within every state, there are some divisions into other units. I will use my own state of Pennsylvania as an example. The Commonwealth is divided into counties, and then into townships, cities, and boroughs. Some of these units are overwhelmingly Red while others are predominantly Blue.

The proposed model envisions a three-tiered governance. Some powers and responsibilities that must be addressed nationally (e.g., interstate highway system, national parks and forests) would continue to reside with the federal government. But many of the powers held by both federal and state authorities would now reside with one of two Spheres. In future chapters, I will offer a suggestion of how that division may look.

---

8 Peter Norton, <u>The US Constitution and Other Key American writings</u>, 2015, Canterbury Classics, page 113.

In this model, cities and some boroughs may want to be part of a Blue Sphere, while townships and other boroughs may want to be part of a Red Sphere. Within each state, there would be regions (I will call them Zones) belonging to each of the two Spheres. Zones could replace counties and perhaps other local units as well.

Just as citizens of Pennsylvania are not bound to follow laws and ordinances issued in Ohio while in Pennsylvania, so the Red Sphere citizens and Blue Sphere citizens would not be bound to the laws and ordinances of the opposite Sphere while in their own Sphere. However, just as a Pennsylvania resident visiting or temporarily residing in Ohio would still need to adhere to the laws of Ohio while in Ohio, so, too, would Blue Sphere residents need to adhere to the laws of the Red Sphere when visiting or residing in areas of that Sphere and vice versa.

For example, coming North on Route 15 from Frederick, Maryland to the Pennsylvania border, the current speed limit is 55 miles per hour. But as soon as one crosses the line, the speed limit becomes 65. Drivers on each side of the border are expected to adhere to that state's limits, regardless of the state of their residency. But Pennsylvanians do not need to adhere to Maryland speed limits while in Pennsylvania.

Using our example, Pennsylvania would consist of both Red Zones and Blue Zones belonging to the respective Spheres. Given the demographics of the Commonwealth, a series of Blue Zones would probably be interspersed within a contiguous Red geographic area consisting of some number of Red Zones.

There would still be room for the state to administer functions that are noncontroversial and of common concern, for example: the regulation of traffic laws and the issuance of driver's licenses.

CHAPTER 3
Creation of this Political Model

First of all, there would need to be some form of constitutional convention to make needed modifications to the current constitution. Article 5 states "The Congress, whenever two thirds of both Houses shall deem it necessary, shall propose Amendments to this Constitution, or, on the Application of the Legislatures of two thirds of the several States, shall call a Convention for proposing Amendments, which, in either Case, shall be valid to all Intents and Purposes, as Part of this Constitution, when ratified by the Legislatures of three fourths of the several States, or by Conventions in three fourths thereof, as the one or the other Mode of Ratification may be proposed by the Congress...."[9] So the Constitution already provides a method for making necessary changes.

Once the modified constitution has been approved, then a balloting would need to be held for all citizens to express their preference as to which Sphere they choose to belong. From here on out, I will refer to those belonging to a Sphere using the term "Member," reserving the word "citizen" for American nationals. A Member is more than a resident and less that a citizen of the country (i.e., an American). One may be a resident anywhere but a Member of only one Sphere.

Areas where clusters of voters choose to belong to the Red Sphere would become Red Sphere areas and areas where clusters of voters

---

choose to belong to the Blue Sphere would become Blue Sphere areas. There will certainly be areas where the mix is so great that no clear distinction can be made. In those cases, I suggest that the decision be made based on simple majority even though any decision will produce contention. There would also need to be a provision for determining to which Sphere areas belong that are not specifically residential (e.g., industrial parks).

It is likely that there will be citizens who find that, out of necessity or choice, they will need to reside in a Zone of a Sphere to which they do not choose to belong. In a future chapter, I will explore an option for how that may be accommodated.

Going forward. after the Spheres have been established and the initial decisions have been made as to which Sphere each Member belongs, there will be a need to allow for changes. I will explore these in a later chapter as well.

Once the Spheres have been geographically determined, they will need to apportion their respective areas into Zones. Assuming no changes will be made to states or state boundaries, these Zones would be defined within each state. Decisions would also need to be made regarding how Zones may expand or reduce their territories or perhaps even apply to become integrated into the other Sphere. These decisions would need to be made as part of the modification to the Constitution.

CHAPTER 4
Possible Governance Under this Model

At the national level, there would still be an executive—continue to call that person President. However, that person's role would be different in that only truly national concerns that cannot be addressed at the Sphere level would be within the national province.

For example, this person would still have oversight of national parks, the FBI, foreign policy, and military, but topics like healthcare/abortion, gun legislation, and law enforcement and perhaps even environmental concerns, would reside with the executives of the Spheres—call them Sphere Executives perhaps.

There would be no need for fights over election procedures and the right to vote, except perhaps in national elections, since the Spheres would assumedly be oriented to the different political alignments that are the origin of many of the policies states are seeking to put in place, which are the responses to the current conflicts.

It would be hoped that these three executives, and especially the two Sphere executives, would seek to work together at least to the degree that governors of various states and the President do so today.

Likewise, there would be a national legislative branch. Since the Spheres and their Zones would be accountable for much of what is the responsibility of both the national and state governments today, this branch would have a much-reduced legislative scope. It may just be a unicameral legislature as Nebraska has.

The current bicameral legislative system was a response to the concerns in colonial times that larger states would dominate smaller states. But the current divide is not between big or small but between political and social philosophies that occur in virtually every state.

Each Sphere would also have its own legislative body, again perhaps unicameral. It may even be practical to adopt a parliamentary system led by a prime minister as executive.

Pennsylvania is an example of a state with two chambers to balance urban and rural interests. But if this model were implemented, these differences would largely disappear. The populations within each Sphere within the state would be fairly homogeneous. There could still be more than one party representing different or specific interests, but the differences would be fairly minor.

In a parliamentary system, the executive comes either from the majority party or through the determination of who would lead a coalition of parties. So, there would be no gridlock resulting from an executive of one party and a legislature of another.

A national judiciary would still exist but would only adjudicate those issues that were reserved to the national government. Otherwise, Sphere courts, including Sphere Supreme Courts, would reach decisions regarding their own Spheres. That may well mean that decisions and interpretations of the Constitution could be quite different in the two Spheres. But there would no longer be a need for the back-and-forth infighting that occurs today between the different philosophical outlooks.

Under the current framework, there is a national capital, Washington DC, and each state has its own capital. Under the model I am proposing, the national capital could continue to be in Washington, but now each Sphere would have a capital. These could also be in buildings within Washington DC. The city of Washington would administer all current city functions but specific buildings would be designated as national or sphere. There may still be state capitals as well. But, as noted above, governmental powers would be dispersed differently than is now the case and the responsibilities of the states would largely be administrative.

How might this work in practice? Let's use the example of health care. Perhaps the Affordable Care Act would be in place for the Blue Sphere Zones along with an expanded Medicare, but not for the Red Sphere. Blue Sphere citizens residing in a Red Sphere Zone would need to comply with the Blue Sphere requirements for coverage and would be insured under those programs, unless they were insured by their employers. Red Sphere citizens would need to be covered by whatever method was adopted by that Sphere, unless they were covered by employers.

As noted previously, there would still be a need for some kind of state governmental structure for those functions that would be utilized by the Zones of each Sphere.

Traffic laws could continue to be determined on a state level. Perhaps a common Department of Transportation would exist that would need to be funded by the state Zones of both Spheres. But the collective Zones of each Sphere in a state would have their own Department of Education and would fund schools in the Zones of that Sphere separately. So, each state would have two Departments of Education but only one Department of Transportation.

One option is for a state legislature to consist of representatives of each Sphere functioning perhaps similarly to how a corporate Board of Directors functions today. Since only the relatively noncontroversial policies like traffic laws and infrastructure repairs would be addressed, there should be less contention than exists today.

Disagreements could be resolved within the Spheres. If there would be disagreement over funding of a bus service, perhaps that funding would be done at a Sphere level rather than a state level. In the case of Pennsylvania, Zones may replace counties, townships, etc.

Perhaps a state executive would be independently elected as governors are today, or perhaps engaged by the Sphere bodies in each state if that does not prove to be too contentious. Since the proposed model suggests the state legislative body would oversee relatively uncontroversial functions such as Departments of Transportation and Departments of Environmental Protection, the state administrative leader could be appointed by this body much as city managers are appointed. The role of this executive would be much like that of a city manager in providing oversite of those departments that provide day-to-day services and ensuring tax dollars devoted to those services are spent correctly.

CHAPTER 5
Economics and Taxes

It is my assumption that those who choose to belong to the Red Sphere will also choose to continue with the current capitalist economic model that they perceive to benefit them adequately.

The foundation of the American economic system was laid by the Scottish social philosopher, Adam Smith, who wrote the ground-breaking work *An Inquiry into the Nature and Causes of the Wealth of Nations* (1776)[10] in which he articulated the principles of the free-enterprise system.

One of the key ideas he stated in his work was of the "invisible hand" that guides the supply and demand in an economy. He believed, *"Every individual…intends only his own gain, and he is in this, as in many other cases, led by an invisible hand to promote an end which was no part of his intention"*[11] In other words, selfish self-interest will lead to the best overall benefit to society as a whole.

Another key idea was his emphasis on free markets. *"In general, if any branch of trade, or any division of labour, be advantageous to the public, the freer and more general the competition, it will always be the more so."*[12]

---

[10] Adam Smith, <u>The Wealth of Nations</u>, CreateSpace Independent Publishing Platform, 2013

[11] Ibid, page 198

[12] Ibid, page 146

But he also believed that individuals had a duty to support the functions of government. *"The subjects of every state ought to contribute towards the support of the government, as nearly as possible, in proportion to their respective abilities...."*[13]

His economic philosophy and assessment of human nature have become so engrained in the cultural mindset of this nation, that they are virtually never questioned. They resulted in the greatest advancements in standard of living and technological progress in the history of humanity.

However, what worked in the simpler times of shopkeepers and small merchants eventually evolved into a system that was dominated by nineteenth century monopolies and powerful trusts like oil and sugar and steel.

The Andrew Carnegies and J.D. Rockefellers built their fortunes, to a greater or lesser degree, by driving smaller concerns out of business and by exploiting labor. This was an age of minimal government oversite and regulation or government controlled by business interests. The abuses eventually led to, among other things, antitrust laws and the rise of labor organizations.

We are experiencing in our time the challenge of income distribution and the accumulation of great wealth by a few as well as negative environmental impacts that are a product of our current economic system.

Those in the Blue Sphere may choose a different model. Because of the vision many of those who would identify themselves with the Blue Sphere have for America, one approach would be to organize businesses around employee-owned cooperatives. There may still be family-owned businesses, but larger enterprises that would be corporations in the Red Sphere could be employee-owned in the Blue Sphere.

In this paradigm, research and development would be funded by the Sphere and then made available for business opportunities within the Sphere. Blue Sphere-owned banks could fund business startups.

---

[13] Ibid, page 366.

This would also alleviate practices today associated with redlining and discrimination. These are just examples of how the two Spheres could evolve economic solutions that benefit their respective Members.

One other option is suggested by Malcom Turnbull, former prime minister of Australia. He proposed that large multinationals would pay tax where they operate and earn profits.[14] These measures could provide municipalities, especially cities, with resources that would enable them to avoid dependencies on wealthy donners.

In the January 17/24, 2022 edition of *Time Magazine*, Leslie Dickstein and Simmone Shah reported on benefactors who provided much-needed funding to a rustbelt city. The monies enable that city to make repairs that they would not have been able to make otherwise. On one hand, the largesse helped to ensure the municipality can balance its annual budget. But on the other hand, the funds came with stipulations that limit what the city council can do. It also resulted in a greater dependency on their donors.[15]

Taxation could occur at several levels as it does today. Most domestic spending would be at the Sphere level. Within the Spheres, the Zones may also have need of taxes as do counties and other municipalities do today. The exception would be if budgets are centralized at the state Sphere level.

While taxes related to real estate, sales taxes, and occupational taxes would be levied and used in the Sphere in which they are collected, income taxes would only be applicable to the specific Sphere. That is to say, tax monies collected in a Sphere would only be utilized in that Sphere. There would be no allocation of tax monies to the other Sphere. Note that Zones within the states could choose to centralize budgets at the state Sphere level.

But as noted earlier, revenues for national expenses such as national parks and interstate highways, the military, and national government would still be collected and spent at a national level.

---

[14] Malcom Turnbull, "A New Tax Deal," <u>TIME</u> August 23/30 2021, page 87

[15] Leslie Dickstein and Simmone Shah, "The Super Rich Stepped in to Save a City. Some Say They Made It Worse" <u>TIME</u>, January 17/24,2021, pages 74-75

As technology progresses, the form that the economy takes may well need to evolve in both Spheres. It is already the case that many jobs that once provided a comfortable income for individuals and families have disappeared forever. And technology as well as artificial intelligence will obviate others in the future.

Among these occupations are assembly-line and factory workers, bus drivers, taxi drivers, truck drivers, phone operators, receptionists, cashiers, and bank tellers.[16] This is by no means an exhaustive list. Even when manufacturing is brought back to the US, automation eliminates a large number of former jobs. And globalization allows jobs to be outsourced to the cheapest locations, as has happened to varying extents to the computer programming occupations. In his article, "China's AI Boom," Kai-Fu Lee remarks that he can foresee a time when robots and AI will take over the manufacturing, design, and delivery and even marketing on most goods. Robots will become self-replicating, and even partially self-repairing. It may be years before these visions of the future enter the mainstream. But China is laying the groundwork right now. [17]

As individuals are replaced with technology, some accommodation will need to be made to enable them to have an income. The solutions for resolving this dilemma may differ by Sphere. For example, the Blue Sphere may choose to go with a minimum income allotment derived from taxing business in that Sphere.

On a small scale, experiments like the Compton Pledge have been conducted to ensure a guaranteed income, but these were derived from private donations. This may also be an option that might work like an on-going GoFundMe account at some level.[18]

There are obviously other ways that a Sphere could generate revenue such as methods that were used to relieve economic distress during the Pandemic of 2020–21, but I will not explore the pros and cons of those here.

---

[16] "What jobs are being taken over by robots and computers?", Computer Hope, March 06, 2020, https://www.computerhope.com/issues/ch001799.htm

[17] Kai-Fu Lee, "China's AI boom," TIME August 23/30 2021, page 78

[18] Abby Vesoulis, and Abigail Abrams, "The Free-Money Experiment," TIME, October 11/18 2021, page 92

CHAPTER 6
Social Issues

"The worst sin toward our fellow creatures is not to hate them, but to be indifferent to them: that's the essence of inhumanity."[19] George Bernard Shaw (England, 1856–1950).

During the Great Depression and again during the 1960s, there were some efforts expended to address the needs of the less fortunate: passage of Social Security and Medicare, Civil Rights and Voting Rights legislation, Medicaid. But for most of our history, Rugged Individualism (the ideal that an individual is self-reliant and independent from outside, usually state or government, assistance) had been the predominate principle that has impelled government policy. It appears that is still the case in this age.

In 1776 the colony of Pennsylvania formed into its own semi-independent state. In the constitution that was written, the former colonists chose to call their new state a Commonwealth. The word was adopted from the British term used by sixteenth century English philosophers like John Locke and Thomas Hobbes for providing for the "common weal" or common good of its citizens.[20]

Yet a 2017 study by the State Health Access Data Assistance Center found that Pennsylvania was 45th in per-capita public health spending.

---

[19] BrainyQuote, https://www.brainyquote.com/quotes/george_bernard_shaw_122419

[20] Editors of Encyclopedia Britannica, "commonwealth," Encyclopedia Britannica, https://www.britannica.com/topic/commonwealth-political-science

This included state support to local health departments and general assistance, which is within the Department of Human Services. In fact, trend lines show a steady decrease in state spending since 2005. Some programs such as paid sick leave are often attacked.[21]

And although Pennsylvania ranks 7th for its average per-pupil funding level,[22] it is in the bottom fifth for how monies are distributed. Districts with high concentrations of poverty are actually receiving *less* money per student than wealthier districts.[23] I can attest that there are many outstanding school districts in the state, but the gap between the number of well-funded and well-supported districts and those that are not continues to be significant.

I use Pennsylvania as a case in point of a trend that is nationwide. America faces challenges in childcare, equable education, housing, law enforcement, a livable wage for many, and access to affordable health care among others. Issues like abortion and immunization have become political issues that cause all dialogue to cease. Instead, we spend effort and money on fighting elections and working to counter the influence of others or in imposing policies on those holding minority views.

If the country could gravitate to separate political spheres, I believe these problems could be addressed as each alignment chooses. The Red Sphere would almost certainly set policies based on the principle of individualism and self-reliance and a conservative-traditional social agenda. Many have done well for themselves and their families this way.

But I believe that the Blue Sphere would be best served with a view

---

21 John I. Micek, "Pa. ranks 45th in the nation in per-capita public health spending," Pennsylvania Capital-Star, July 24, 2019, https://www.penncapital-star.com/commentary/pa-ranks-45th-in-the-nation-in-per-capita-public-health-spending-report-wednesday-morning-coffee/#:~:text=Now%2C%20this%20morning%2C%20according%20to,per%2Dcapita%20public%20health%20spending.

22 "Per Pupil Spending by State 2022," US Education Spending Statistics, 2022, https://worldpopulationreview.com/state-rankings/per-pupil-spending-by-state.

23 "National Study Finds Pennsylvania's Education Funding Gap Among Nation's Worst," The Public Interest Law Center, April 1, 2015, https://www.pubintlaw.org/cases-and-projects/national-study-finds-pennsylvanias-education-funding-gap-among-nations-worst-calls-disparity-devastatingly-large/

toward cooperation and collective well-being. When Americans think of Socialism, they think of the Soviet Union or China or even North Korea but very seldom of Scandinavia or even the mixed economy of Germany.

Germany has indisputably the strongest and most prosperous economy in Europe. Like the United States, it is based on free enterprise / capitalism. But it also offers a broad range of benefits to protect its citizens. Among these benefits is included nursing care, a family allowance system to help families provide for their children and the so-called mother's pension, intended to serve as an acknowledgment of mothers' work raising children. This is on top of unemployment insurance, insurance for the permanently disabled, and workers' pensions. Of course, these all require tax levels that we have not found acceptable to date. But since the 1800s, Germany has sought to ensure security for all of its citizens as well as supporting economic development.[24]

In this chapter, I want to explore several social issues that have deeply divided us. The first I want to address is the issue of abortion. It is clear that each side has deeply held beliefs about the right for women to decide versus the sanctity of the life of the unborn. It is interesting to me that in many cases this sanctity is not extended to death penalty cases. It is often argued on the basis of innocence of the unborn versus the guilt of criminals. This suggests to me that some lives are viewed as more sacred than others. It is not my intention to weigh in on this controversy. Rather, I would like to question the lack of concern for the fetus once it is born.

Within the right to life movement, I have heard few calls for child support. Wealthier women can afford to go where abortions are available, but poorer women are often left with no options. And the children born to them often face lives of deprivation and abuse. It is no surprise that many of these infants grow up facing a bleak future in situations

---

[24] "Strong Welfare State, Facts About Germany, https://www.tatsachen-ueber-deutschland.de/en/germany-glance/strong-welfare-state

that are both dangerous and unhealthy. And it is not surprising that these environments often engender crime. For every child that makes it out of this environment, many, many more face lives of hopelessness.

I believe that even if abortion is declared to be illegal, the Blue Sphere would be in the position to provide the support to these newborns that the Red Sphere most likely would not be willing to do.

Second, like abortion, the issue of law enforcement is seen quite differently by the two paradigms. I find it interesting that in my suburban neighborhood, I find signs on lawns for either Black Lives Matter and the litany of concerns about science, immigrants, women's rights, diversity, etc. or the signs supporting local police. But I have yet to find a yard where both signs are displayed. It appears that if you support local police, you do not also support other issues like Black Lives Matter.

I am also aware of the political bent of many if not most of the people who display one sign or the other. What I have noticed is that protests around defunding police (which in most cases is really about funding sources that would be first responders rather than police) seem to occur in areas where police behavior is not an issue.

To my knowledge, it has been almost exclusively in urban areas that incidents have arisen. Most rural areas and even most suburban areas have not experienced these occurrences or at least not with the same frequency. Cities, suburbs, and rural areas each have their own challenges. Yet it appears to me that many communities are condemning choices that do not affect them at all.

There is another side to this issue. In 1887 John Emerich Edward Dalberg-Acton (Lord Acton) wrote to Bishop Creighton his now famous line, "Power tends to corrupt and absolute power corrupts absolutely."[25] In June of 2020, the *New York Times* published an article on how police unions resist attempts at any kind of reform, even in the cases of clear misconduct and sometime behavior that borders on the criminal.[26]

---

[25] Wikipedia, https://en.wikipedia.org/wiki/John_Dalberg-Acton,_1st_Baron_Acton
[26] "Fierce Protectors of Police Impede Efforts at Reform," New York Times, Section A, Page

Policing is clearly a necessary but potentially dangerous profession, especially but not exclusively, in urban areas. And those who serve deserve our thanks and support. However, Lord Acton wrote in the same letter to the bishop that people in power positions should be held to the same standards as all others. Police are clearly in a position of power.

In 1970, the American journalist Howard Sochurek interviewed an English couple who had moved to East Berlin for political reasons, John and Georgia Peet. During the interview, Georgia, a former Romanian who had been interned in a German concentration camp, made the following observation, "I am still struck by the way power changes people. It absolutely corrupts them when they have total control over their fellow beings [as in that camp]. [27]

Given our current climate, I cannot imagine any way that the two positions—police reform, in whatever form that may take, and affirmation of police in the position they now hold— can ever be reconciled.

However, in the case of the two Spheres, I believe that each Sphere would be in the position to adopt those laws that would best suit their positions. This could well mean, at least initially, that a significant percentage of police would choose to take employment in the Red Sphere, since I assume the Red Sphere would continue to support the status quo. But this could give the Blue Sphere the opportunity to address concerns in a way that could result in less conflict.

Third, I find it interesting that the name "Comanche" comes from the Ute word *k mantsi* meaning "enemy, stranger." [28] Some scholars have stated that humans have been tribal since our early beginnings. I believe this is no less true today than it has been in the past. And I believe this is the origin of prejudices of all kinds. People tend to associate with others much like themselves. And the divisions within our society have

---

1, June 7, 2020, https://static01.nyt.com/images/2020/06/07/nytfrontpage/scan.pdf

[27] Howard Sochurek, "Berlin on both sides of the Wall," National Geographic, January 1970, page 23

[28] Edward Sapir, "Southern Paiute Dictionary." 1931 Reprinted in 1992 in: <u>The Collected Works of Edward Sapir, X, Southern Paiute and Ute Linguistics and Ethnography</u>. Ed. William Bright. Berlin: Mouton deGruyter.

simply accelerated this trend. Unfortunately, this situation has evolved into a strong us vs. them—we good, they bad—dynamic that generates intolerance and often hostility.

The issues of race-ethnicity, gender equality or at least equity, and sexual identify have been at the center of power struggles around rights that go back and forth depending on who wins elections. I do not see an end in sight as long as the two visions for America are in constant competition. But I believe that the Spheres would be the resolution to much of the conflict. As noted in early chapters, some would need to live and work in a Sphere to which they don't belong, but over time I believe most could migrate to the Sphere to which they have an affinity.

While there are certainly many other issues I could explore, the last one that I want to address in this chapter is housing and homelessness. I take it for granted that the reader is well aware of the increase in homelessness that was generated by the economic challenges during the COVID outbreak of 2020 and beyond. But COVID only aggravated a situation that has been building for some time.

At heart, the issue is economic. Those who own rental properties do so to produce income. In a sense, tenants are simply a source of money. Likewise, builders build to make money. In a free-enterprise system, housing is left to the capitalist system. The motivation is primarily, if not exclusively, to generate wealth, not to ensure that everyone has adequate housing.

In some areas of the country like the San Francisco Bay area, the problem is aggravated by the price of land and property. Those with the jobs and incomes that enable them to afford to live in the area seek what service industry employees offer. But those employees do not make incomes that enable them to live in the area. And those who have expensive homes and condos do not want low-income housing to be built in their area because it would lower property values.

If the Blue Sphere adopts a communal philosophy, tax money could be used to address at least some of these problems in a way that could accommodate both needs (for example via mass transit and fast trains to and from less expensive living areas). This is money that in our current environment is simply not available. As I have mentioned before, to resolve most of the economic challenges, it would require taxation levels that those who share a Red Sphere philosophy are not prepared to bear in this age. Public housing has a bad name, but if the profit incentive were removed from the solution and the focus was on ensuring adequate housing for all, then much of the problem could be resolved.

Let me use an example. Without identifying specific locations, there are cases of trailer communities that have banded together to buy out the former owners and create community parks. These parks are organized as cooperatives with members owning their own trailer or mobile home and everyone contributing to the costs of maintenance and upkeep of the park as a whole.

The Sphere could provide the money and perhaps the organization to produce collective structures that people could rent. But unlike the current climate, the renters would not be forced out because they lost the means to pay. Yes, there would be cases of misuse and abuse, but policies could be adopted to deal with these if the concern is for the welfare of those living in the Sphere.

I am not seeking to provide ultimate solutions to all of these challenges, only to offer possibilities that could become the basis for dialogue and resolution.

CHAPTER 7
Some Possible Scenarios

These scenarios represent what I perceive to be some of the most obvious if the model were to be implemented.

Scenario 1: Becoming a Member of a Sphere

Initially when the model is first implemented, individuals would need to decide to which Sphere they will belong. They will also need to determine to which Zone within the selected Sphere they will become a Member. As noted previously, it may be possible for different members of a household to choose to be Members of different Spheres.

At the time of implementation parents and custodians will need to determine to which Sphere their charges will also belong temporarily until they reach adulthood and decide for themselves. This will be especially important for households that are split between the Spheres. The same is true for children born after the initial changes. In these cases, it may be necessary through court battles to determine a primary caregiver who would decide for their charges.

When a child reaches adulthood, he or she will then go through the same process as any other adult in choosing Memberships. The same is true for immigrants who become citizens.

Scenario 2: Household Members are Members of Different Spheres.

There will certainly be cases where individuals will choose to reside in a Zone of a Sphere to which they do not belong. This may occur because of workplace requirements or locations, or because members of a household are Members of different Spheres. It may also occur because of decisions related to purchases of property or caregiver needs.

In these cases, the non-Sphere citizens will be bound to all laws and ordinances of that Zone/Sphere but will continue to enjoy the rights and benefits of the Zone/Sphere to which they belong.

To further clarify this situation, I will offer an example. Jane Doe is married to John Doe and they both live in the Red Sphere. John chose to be a Member of the Blue Sphere but Jane chose to be a Member of the Red Sphere. Jane has private insurance but John is covered by the universal healthcare plan established by his Sphere. Each person votes in the Sphere to which they belong, perhaps remotely if necessary.

Utility bills would be paid to the utilities that service that address. Any fees or taxes that relate to vehicles or statewide infrastructure costs would be paid to the state, unless determined otherwise. Of course, rent for apartments (especially in the Red Sphere) would be paid to landlords.

Scenario 3: Changing Sphere Membership

In the case where a Member of one Zone chooses to move to another Zone in the same Sphere, the change would be as simple as what occurs today when a person moves from one county to another. The rules for moving to a different state also would be similar.

However, some individuals will determine it is in their interest to seek to change Sphere Membership because there is a perception that there are more or better opportunities, for whatever reason, in the other Sphere. I assume each Sphere will set its own membership requirements based on what is defined in the Constitution. So, it is possible that an individual seeking to change Membership would be denied for one reason or another.

That does not mean those individuals could not reside in the other Sphere. They would still enjoy all the benefits of American citizenship but not the advantages or specific benefits (e.g., healthcare policies) that Membership in that Sphere would provide.

Scenario 4: Law Enforcement

Most law enforcement would be conducted at the Sphere/Zone level. That means that local ordinances as well as policing practices would be determined by the respective jurisdictions.

Sphere laws regarding criminal offenses and punishments would replace some of the corresponding national laws.

Police contracts as well as police oversight would be the responsibly of the local Zone unless a unform code were to be enacted across one or the other of the Spheres. I believe this would resolve the disputes over funding or defunding local police as well as arguments over police oversight. Each Sphere or Zone within a Sphere could decide how they would want to approach these and similar issues.

Of course, the rules governing pursuit that apply today across state lines would apply across Zones within a state or across states. If police are in pursuit of a suspect and that individual crosses Zone lines, the police would be authorized to continue the pursuit. And if a suspect of a crime committed in a Zone of one Sphere is found in the Zone of the other Sphere, the same rules governing interstate investigation and extradition that are currently in force would also apply.

CHAPTER 8
Conclusion

Many will think me naïve even to suggest that a change this major would be possible. As Niccolò Machiavelli. Italian Renaissance philosopher, wrote in 1513 in his work *The Prince*: "It ought to be remembered that there is nothing more difficult to take in hand, more perilous to conduct, or more uncertain in its success, than to take the lead in the introduction of a new order of things.

"Because the innovator has for enemies all those who have done well under the old conditions, and lukewarm defenders in those who may do well under the new. This coolness arises partly from fear of the opponents, who have the laws on their side, and partly from the incredulity of men, who do not readily believe in new things until they have had a long experience of them."[29]

Even then, it was understood how difficult social change can be. However, to paraphrase a local radio station's comment about music, everything was once new. It will not be a simple matter to evolve the country into this model, but it has become increasingly clear that we have become what is quite possibly irreconcilably divided. This divide is not along geographical lines, nor is it along strictly class lines but along ethnic and philosophical lines.

---

[29] Machiavelli, Niccolò, <u>The Prince</u>, chapter VI, Project Gutenberg, https://www.gutenberg.org/files/1232/1232-h/1232-h.htm

We waste so much time and money trying to prevent our cultural opponents from gaining any advantage or having their policies implemented—time and money better spent on real issues related to quality of life. Even a simple matter of wearing a mask or not wearing a mask during a pandemic becomes a badge of political identify.

If we are to resolve this conflict and progress as a society, we need to find a way to accommodate the incompatible. Creating two different Spheres in which we could live side by side in different political and social paradigms could be the solution that would allow us as a country to face the foreign and domestic challenges that threaten us all.

For every Elon Musk or Jeff Bezos or Steve Jobs, there are tens of thousands just hanging on, with many more struggling to maintain an adequate standard of living, not knowing what tomorrow will bring. And this is not to mention the countless number who have been left out in the cold enduring a day-to-day struggle just to survive.

I believe the efforts to force change and redistribute wealth are largely a waste of time. It only yields an endless struggle between those I will refer to as idealists and those with wealth and power and with many in the middle taking sides for one reason or another. Whether we refer to liberals and conservative or progressives and traditionalists, what we wind up with is an endless tug-of-war that produces, at best, transitory progress or regression and at worst violence and conflict.

Efforts like we have seen in 2021 to "stack the deck" for future elections to ensure party dominance may be successful for some period of time. But inevitably the dynamics will eventually change because of demographic changes or changes in political positions. The immediate danger is that these efforts will result in violence and social upheaval that would certainly weaken America no matter which side prevailed.

Because the two primary visions for America are so different, I see no way that efforts to bring about some kind of compromise will ever succeed. As I have suggested throughout this presentation, the only viable alternative, in my opinion, is to allow the two visions to evolve side by side in separate Spheres.

This will probably mean that most rural areas will chose to be part of the Red Sphere along with most of those who see themselves or seek to become entrepreneurs. And many urban areas, along with areas populated by various ethnic groups, would choose to be part of the Blue Sphere. This will leave suburban areas to split one way or another, based on their political and social affinities and ethnic makeup.

Make no mistake, I believe that the Blue Sphere, were it to be created, would be, at least initially, at a distinct disadvantage economically. To achieve most of the goals I set out in this proposal, it will require teamwork and sacrifice but most of all patience. In previous chapters, I argued some steps that I believe would need to be taken in order to address some of the imbalances, both economic and social, that we experience today.

In any case, the two competing visions could go their own way. There would probably be some migrations in the early stages because many will find themselves residing in a sphere in which they do not want to remain. But the overall result would be a society at peace while still offering a nation united in the face of foreign challenges.

If we are willing to take the risks and expend the effort this change would entail, then we could emerge a stronger nation. Our future and our children's future depend on our finding a way out of the conflict that threatens to tear our country apart. Perhaps this solution would provide just such an answer. The next steps depend upon our willingness to make this change to end the ceaseless conflicts that plague our society.